I0223669

A Ticket to Trilce

Also by M.T.C. Cronin

POETRY

Zoetrope – we see us moving
the world beyond the fig
Everything Holy
Mischief-Birds
Bestseller
Talking to Neruda's Questions
    [Respondiendo a las Preguntas de Neruda (Spanish/English)]
    [Controcanto - Il Libro Delle Domande di Neruda (Italian/English)]
My Lover's Back - 79 Love Poems
The Confetti Stone and other poems
beautiful, unfinished - PARABLE/SONG/CANTO/POEM
<More or Less Than> 1-100
The Ridiculous Shape of Longing - New & Selected Poems (Macedonian/English)
The Flower, the Thing
Notebook of Signs (& 3 Other Small Books)
Our Life is a Box / Prayers Without a God
How Does a Man Who is Dead Reinvent His Body? The Belated Love Poems
        of Thean Morris Caelli (co-written with Peter Boyle)
Irrigations (of the Human Heart) - Fictional Essays on The Poetics
        of Living, Art & Love
The World Last Night [metaphors for death]
in possession of loss
The Law of Poetry
Causal - speaking the future
Sometimes the Soul
God is Waiting in the World's Yard
what we have except when we are lost (co-written with Maria Zajkowski)

ESSAYS

Squeezing Desire Through a Sieve - Micro-essays on Judgement & Justice

M.T.C. Cronin

A Ticket to Trilce

Shearsman Books

First published in the United Kingdom in 2021 by
Shearsman Books
PO Box 4239
Swindon
SN3 9FN

Shearsman Books Ltd Registered Office
30–31 St. James Place, Mangotsfield, Bristol BS16 9JB
(this address not for correspondence)

www.shearsman.com

ISBN 978-1-84861-750-6

Copyright © M.T.C. Cronin, 2021.
The right of M.T.C. Cronin to be identified as the author
of this work has been asserted by her in accordance with the
Copyrights, Designs and Patents Act of 1988.
All rights reserved.

ACKNOWLEDGEMENTS
Extracts (some under different titles) have appeared in the following:
Dispatches from the Poetry Wars; Famous Reporter, Four W; Green Left Weekly;
Gutcult; Hermes; Jacket; Laika Poetry Review; Mad Hatter's Review;
Tangent (University of Sydney Women's Anthology, 2000).

LXIII was originally published as 'An Exotic Garden Viewed at Different
Levels' written after the painted door of the same name by Donald Friend, was
performed at the *Parallel Visions* Exhibition, Art Gallery of NSW, 2003 and
hung alongside the painting which inspired it. It was published in the book,
Parallel Visions/Parallel Poetry (Art Gallery of NSW, Sydney, 2003).

XXXIV is dedicated to Jim Elkins.

Extracts from *A Ticket to Trilce* were nominated
for a Pushcart Prize, USA, 2006.

Cover design by Tim Cronin.

Any apparent spelling mistakes in the book are intentional.

A Ticket
to
Trilce

I on one undated day, then
19 April – 24 April 2006
and a frisking on 29 April same year

With thanks to César Vallejo's Trilce
&
to the authors of various English versions
(Clayton Eshleman; Rebecca Seiferle; Peter Boyle;
and Michael Smith & Valentino Gianuzzi)

Pay for watermellows with ticker tards;
unhabit the pub late and pry back.
Two or three sweet sad words
and you can think of nothing else!

Have you not been considering
the mirrors in your eyes;
not been wondering what is the name
of the city in your mind?

I

Mummy! Mummy! Mummy!
Backwards you're born. Two different ways this is so.

    The island is not what you leave but what you inherit.
You go on alone.
With no consideration the future accepts only you.
Inconsiderate time, liquid and insular.
From Australia to Peru it ignores and welcomes.
Welcomes and ignores.
Just like the mother gives birth to the most perpetual
                dying. Din. The flattest B's.

    At what time the pivot on which you swing
and listen to the sound made by paradox?
PLOP!

    Whether you think it's a pelican or a gannet
in Alcatraz hasn't to do with here or there.
Nor *nor*.

II

Temporal lobe lobe.

Here and now is the joke of being.
How it got stuck in the experience that we
feel feel feel feel.

Pin prick prick.

Scratching for blood in the bloodless.
Bleached mouth alive around the
word word word word.

What is it? It it.

Up against this.
Both fully dressed as if they
could could could could.

And yet yet.

The poor brain's always trying.
Copying the little bit into a new bit
that's that's that's thatIS.

III

I'm forty-three
and still waiting for my mother
to come back.
It's still dark.

My mother and father were always at work.

Tim and Miss X and Jennie
sit on the step and draw names
in the dust.
Four letter words are giggles (Bald Iggles.)
Across the hill that never comes closer
the road, the soundless road.
All eyes travelling.
All little arms entwined
for a hundred years too late.

The story is they're dead. One
can always make the others
cry. The old babysitter gets the soap
to wash out their mouths.
Put your foot through the wall.
Tell the old bitch she's a goner.

No wait! The arms of her,
the arms of her are coming
to hold us, hold us in the sun
of grease-marks smelling
liks soup tunes rice and nostalgia's
                              never-leaves.

Tim, the one, Jennie?

We're alone all in the dream
that won't stay the same.
We grow old together in the dark.

IV

The metal of the truck's gate
hits his head, closes his eyes
with the same sound the sky makes
coming down on the tree-tops.
Mother hems it.
She can hear an eggshell cracking
as the spirit   releases.

I undid the chains, followed orders.
Opened his face with the weight
of a thumb. Second-born.
Leaving prints all
                    up and down
the cross so shock
could marry the game.
Withdrawing mother from the silence.

So what!
He got a metal pea that travelled
his discoloured cheek for the next loose
decade.

The scar was a song.
Song-like-jelly.   Song like her hand
tracing this massive eternal welt. (Courage-song.)

V

Group of the wrong number.
Instable. Too many to climb a cupboard at once
or fit on the back of a bird.
From the plate grows a jungle of beans, the universe
folds back again – both halves – to let them see in.

Mmmm. A voice-man. He's the one.
Trapped the listeners in a family made
out of hypocritical fast cars.
Mmmm. The whistle transcends the horn.
Chrome collapses him. Till change flies.

The three little creatures
set up a bird-song.
Forever makes no sense.
1 they sent out the window on a rope.
0 was heard.
Still was survival against the odd.

Group of politics and love.

VI

Putting on my glissade and frisson!
Filthy from being left in the dark.
From crawling around looking for me
in time I've not entered.
Bloody anticipation soils my heart,
makes me mean.

    All the water-carriers
have smelt my ungratefulness, know
I'd sell them to the devils
for a chance to fly.
Yet they laugh at those
who become yourself.
        They know the Goddess of Wheat
and remain sealed.

    If I knew how to open them
I could get the secrets and dress
like a nightstand. The world
would be that small because happy
happy it would always be me.
        HOW COULD IT NOT!
My berry soul would squash
and kold juice of chaos spread over the lot.

VII

Every outroad led me back inside.
As usual.
Out I'd go and come back in.
In and out; out and in.

Nobody seemed to care much for my safety.
All the corners backed off.
I huddled bare-bottomed into them
and they halved themselves rawly.

The magnitude of it!
Shouts passed down the street
until they reached my door
like an axe with its collapsible journey
                                        over.
No bells, no eyes, no ringing open.
But 44 676 000 minutes in an antswarm
endeared themselves like cripples
to the smoking years between 2006 and 1921.

VIII

Tomorrow is the only day before the day
after tomorrow and today it's the only day
you can buy a ticket for.

Where's the booth that homes the seller
with a double skin sewn
from what we wasted
of our erotic eternity?

Should be fixed like a dog that ruts
too much if they're all given licence
to a tomorrow that stops right there.
This is what I think, anchordrop,
looking at myself in the lavatory mirror
as the sewer echoes down my back
as if it had flipped my own lips.

IX

All over the sheets and out on the grass
blokes are at it as if God
didn't have a sense of humour.
No provocation or blow required.
Any calyx
might be an entry point.

They mix up language with thrust
and grunt through the fists.
Little big animals.
Hair and lip exchange.
Bookwriters as after it as the next man
for they're all missing
     the soft bits.

They won't go soft on it though.
Like bulls of Zawoolp
they know it's charge or die!
Line up the hole and head for it. Gulp
for gulp! The most radical work
is co-founded. Con.

Confound it! She's a she!
And their souls try the female way.

X

Incorporate the stone.
It's all that's clean.
In the month of your birth – the same month –
count to thirteen by ten and by three
and laugh all the way through happiness dying.
Soul and all finally!

How met!
How contrary!
How hopeless!

How whale is the ocean
and how dove, the sky.
And if it's a cube, then whale, wing,
dove and all monotony, the saddle!

Ten only gets you to ten
when the god is fourteen
you can already be too pregnant.
Gestate the stone
and give birth to absence!

No violence ensues.
Following such sickness the patient will sit up
(grinly oblivous) into a mixture of tranquillity and peacocks.

XI

Today I ran into the boy
I loved from ten to twenty
and handed over all my dreams,
spiders beyond the human eye.

His name mocked me with a new name,
too small to see, to step on.
He was old without being old,
old to me and tainted
        as if he had drowned
        in a separate future.

        "I still love you"
he tells me and my stomach chews up
my stomach from a distance.
        He loves / am I.
        He loves / I got.

A year of afterlust vultures us
as if we were dead adders, as if
we had died like generals
pronounced perpendicular to the direction.

XII

The flies here are tralaticious.
Untouchable during interviews.
Perched, unironically, on the lips.

Gravity is called for
– especially when many have died –
but doesn't seem to work
on any of Newton's bones.

It is certain that tonight they'll be jigging.
Natural disasters just another excuse
for the drink. Its spike.
Showdown! Banged down on the bar, five by five.

XIII

Your sex doesn't bear my thinking.
It has a mud of its own.
Prickly winning wars.
My heart is ensavaged by its fat Winter,
how in one thought it tosses forward
the ancient. (Tosses like a goat.)

Your sex is the purple flower coming up the hill
chanting its muscle, coming up through
the womb dripping God.
It kills you!
Some kind of beast stretched out in you
has forgotten pleasure,
never knew conscience.

Oh comes before Pee in our alphabet.
Willhe is all you think about now.

Nahhsapwarrr...

XIV

My heresy is obvious.
It lets some air in, some collisions.

That the praise browns like droughted grass.

Then messages lassoo my heart in chains.

That expensive artwork winks.

Then the risley spoon scoops at their bums.

That seems not how it appears.

Crève-

cœur.

But I've come from Sydney to Maleny.
I've searched for the elusive platypus wage.

XV

In that funnel where we lived together
the machine now churns forming ruffles,
noise like a saltatory insect,
spinning my organs into the numb.

Why do you knot drop by these days
becoming crimson in their complaint
and entreaty?
It's one thing to read, but another entirely
to mouth words that have since been roasted
to crispness.

I remember your well-developed skeleton
causing your coat to project behind.
You acted so gravely.

By whatever means I punish myself
with memories strewn like suddens
over the sacrificial victims
of this and all nights that
love   to   love.

XVI

My only faith has been the gut-feeling.
So thankyou embedded truths
and zero information.
It seems I'm to be saved for lies, saved
not to be overcome by lies, by the unverifiable –

The bank violation, the criminous clock,
the purplish suburbs, those hyper-local
cramps with their vicious habit
of biting the manager –

all have been surpassed by my impatience,
the point at which I'll decide anything,
the curvy schemed bits kept
for their uncrowned mates.

My lame faith has been like reading
a gut-feeling.

So! Unread!

XVII

The diadem spider
applies itself to the garden.
Diaheliotropic could split death
into the offender and the washerwoman.

There's too many jobs this morning!
The brain-cache's full!
Petals separate desire into
the determination and the description.
More or less is as precise as measuring.

The nasturtiums' green flat faces
stick together, surveying what's fixed.
Who knows the unison!?
Could be a symptom of the branch...

There's a cross-magnetic month
that hitches diamonds onto every finger.
It has daily medicine and a series of teeth.
Believe me! With effort.

Do you??

XVIII

Welcome to my calls, said the well.
Cell of love, of thee who was born here,
counting and absorbing the numbers.

What a humble vitality prenates itself
in what is desinent, in any place
where untame death lies highly prized.

And trapped.
By possible keys and more.
Even those unencountered, those slantwise,
fallen through the grate of smiles
by the surveyor who later
expanded his wings like a bird.

Ah these things we use for walls
when the walls fall down!
Dissentient walls.
Incivil to every mother who discharges love
as if from a sponge.
In the walls' damage deprived of no neglect.

Like a controlling planet
I roll around in here
expressing the wall in my cells.
Calls in well. Like yorsef in the pupil of another's eye.
Wall s of cell s. (Separate s's.) Some body diss embly.

XIX

St Sebastian, Friend of Tom & Federico, poor fellow,
your wounds make you more beautiful than Christ or a woman.

Those arrow-headed holes have attracted like orifices
the sucked-back-in words of poets, the sting!
the prick!
the point!

With their dental phrases, thick meanings,
treacherous arguable second sight,
they see you with chin resting on your chest –
Oh!
        The crown of his head…

I think they rather fancied you *before*
they committed their wives to the asylum.

I know, if they could, they would have poked a finger
into your bloody dimples (sticky as honeycomb);
would have lifted your head with a finger
placed delicately under your chin;
and would have kissed your red mouth.

Like honeymooners…

XX

Agate and agate mate in the earth'sjaw.
even the smile of the sun eggs them
as if it was the appearance of a prince.

Meanwhile, the pople make a mess.
Cease to profess the day too short
to fit in their ambitions, lose
                                   sometimes,
their nature and property,
by other arrangements
plan all kinds of new independences.

Suffering bandaids for the suffering.

See how much displeasure needs covering.
How unsettled we are.
Not even the gemstones' enthusiasm
can prevent the flow of urine.
Today, leg broken, I howl.
Tomorrow, leg sure, I howl.

And toes. Behold the toes
blistered by bad repute and picnics.
Emboxed I am. Every limb suddenly appearing.
The grandmother and the infant examine the small one's
rotten foot: one, two, three, seven, eight
46 – this one needs the creamery,
hurting me much with bad scratch,
it's wasted if it doesn't st
                         i.ck

XXI

Between feversfingers fidgeting life goes on.
The fico is given again and again
as if contempt rode a wheel.
So without changing position I fall again:

                                        poor me.

The vicious physicious has recommended
that I take nothing; that what felled me
the first time, all those years ago,
is in the ring again waiting the punch.
Do you believe it?

Mr Rot. Old BodyRot. He's back.
That fiddle-faddler. That dragging-himself-
thru-mybones disgusterama.

I've loved him with a hypochondriac trust
for relieving me of the world with general nervous restlessness.
Pah! How slenpid. I think I'll put on my spotty pyjamas!

XXII

Fi donc! All you judges with dunces
in your fingertips, all called *Grande Pere*.
The not very serious life you can find me in
is hilariously underdone so that I'm
changing my name back to Maggot! What it
never was. What the kids call anyway. Fibbers!

Of late the old lies reel silk, dress torsos
and go fore- and aft-ing to me they
forsee (and foresaw). Contrived antecedently
a guilty point with my head atop it.

What's the history?
There was the underinfluence.
The crash.
The stolen stencils (and a toy as well).
The Italian gigolo chef.
Some now famous.
Rest is exhausted by the prepuce pulled back
to reveal these gamin crimes.
No edge withstands what it withstands.
The God of Foreskite ogles my act
of staring open-mouthed, compares

my sleight-of-hand with the nightingale's
note. Says, you Junkman! Me
and my fellow would-be influencers
will doom-pronounce you. See justice
through your opera-glasses! Clinging!

XXIII

Mother's the greatest fiduciary.
More herself than she's ever managed to be.

She embeds us in the truth.
Got duffed with us the same way.
Bang! Bang! Bang! (Just outside of two years
crawling one and then another, then Jennie,
the actrine, pretty as a nectarine.)

Up the ladder you went with your hammer
and inserted the ceiling (with roof attached)
into the space threatening our soft fonts.
Down the ladder you came with a prefabricated
stallion and cow, with your four uppermost
valves opening and closing on ripe information.

Now you're a juke-box in the yard
with the little jujubes who just keep on
being born, jumping more guns than you
ever did the first time round.
Too much safety makes us wary
and the inside of your ears are swollen
by the history that's been forced in.
History causes a reaction, or at least
whatever wild percent is mixed
with the braincream into a junket.
Oh jugal experiences and stories!

But you're not dead yet!
As they say. As they said.
There's the laundry to fold
and the earth to connect
and the cat food to wipe

and the standing for a constant
and the eight syllables to imitate
and there's us, you haven't
forgotten us, have you mum?

XXIV

The little celebration shall be in the graveyard
because there is the most
beautiful tree.

It grows like a water-jar
with an orange spurge
and shits its sap on the tombs
turning like a kaleidoscope
of obsequies.

The small children
shall fill the cemetery with inconsolable singing.

A birthday.

XXV

As a pineapple – fleshy fruit formed
from a crowd of flowers – are the palatial
consonants and sisterly bugs and creepers
resembling any of our better arch-priests.

None have gone far enough
to hit brotherly love and most of their
states of thriving have come out
with no better than inspissated lettuce
juice. The refugees
are confined to the refuges
and the poor to the tingle
of poverty.
Thous! Three cheers! Olé!

The leafhoppers know when the leaf vibrates
too roughly, springing aboard
the philosophy to jail, sing-sing
the threnody of a bred compassion
(only take it out when you want to use it!).
Woops and whups to the bakers
who want to fuck bakers and ex-
communicating hints to the money-
immune. Whoobub and whommle
to any inverting the dish which awaits
the coin.

And so minute black insects crawl across
their unhurt hearts in a game of hidey.

XXVI

There are the lines drawn
that join into one big
                line
until we're living in a sausage-skin.
The parliament has even made it law.
We are a single whiteness.

        We care not to care.
Mend any broken fences
                undelayably. Painful
                inflammatory
digits are lopped. Few of us confess
at the gallows. Why would we?
It only makes a hissing sound like air
leaving a balloon or a snake that's been stepped on.
Our hearts more brain than hearts.

        Our protervity does not become clear
to us even peeking upwards to check
how close to our heads is the heavy
Northern bum which thus seated
on the toilet of us rather reads cartoons
                than the gospels of James the Less.

        What sticks out of the anus
is a man.
Then another. They're all men!
                Chocolate coated. Dying on the inside.
                Protruded because they can't stay.
                They must go!

        Straight through our skulls

like commodities we opened up
like commodes for.
                    Beasticles!

        But we act like prototypes.
We love it.
Slutty protozoa produced by a gross spore.
The big monkey demands pander-
monium and we stick our tongues
up the shoot.

XXVII

Page ripped by memory –
those sharp bones. Stop reading!
Come in from the ritual
and drink reality's cruel soup.
What you did was real!

Don't tell me that!
I take reproaches to the camomile
where they might be strangled into sleep,
where the past is tucked headlong.

Stop waiting for me!
I am present-afflicted and can't
go back to the shallow waters
of was.

But the sorrow-lulling drug-taker –
the scaffolder of dreams
in my viscera taunts:
'Floating kidney, remember us. Fall. Fall.'

XXVIII

The degustation is afoot and mouth and I
have been invited. Travelling towards
one Pole for forty minutes and I'm a-mutter
in the fashionable roastnrant
where they eat slowly.

But oh! How to eat what I
have not learned. Each pea-
sized attempt ends in another journey,
subterranean and neoteric.
The food is cool. Slightly.

Neon lamps announce the house
to us as tongue-by-tongue it
restaurantizes our fortunes.
Cookie cookie cookie buzzes
at us all unaccompanied,
the lone wolf and the lollipop lady
hungry and lonesome as the young man
recently leaving his mother's house
to find human flesh as meal.

So much grief and sadness
and borborygmui.
Pimientos de Padron and the issue
from an organic goat's tit.
Powrrr.
Flans tarts abdominally glans.

How to eat this sweet breath
exhaled chiefly chefly
when all that awaits in my home
is a can in darkness, abominable Alaska.

XXIX

The buzz is bored.
The breathing red ball bounces into the frame.

Speculation is certain
as the boing does fall in a homeringing walk.
Nothing is created in now
which still has some more to rest.

As it rools that way it tells me
something about a log – the old almost-corpse.

Take care of it or disappearance beats death.

XXX

Lover is chilli-bottling at two
in the afternoon,
bottling chillis
as pure as the driven rice.

Multix disposable gloves, thin as surgery,
stop the burn at some point
before it stops.
Vinegar bapsizes restruby.

Lungfish fingers and toes –
courtesty of the radial gene –
can't touch me for a week just in case
the neotoxin has entered there, masturbatory exercise
                    which leaves my voice
almost empty.

I need a person!
Cloyhoneyripefruitingratiatingtalcumdustedsugarlogged
daintynibblynarrowsweetandhugged
for the poor space
between charming and enamoured.
He's out of action at two in the bloody afternoon!

XXXI

A body of bees has broken up the cuddlerush.

Hope is like a sting, ongoing.
When it is not this it is God, a startled pressure.
Felt in the knees.
In the offshoot as the colony progresses.
Turnishings in the sun
felt as unseen pleasures.

Fate is swaraj, a self-government.
Young swans returning
with the ancient Greek trumpet
to toot.

God is only one of two hundred.
The only one we remember.
But he doesn't know how heavy babies are
and is not an animal you can really
                        touch.
In every knot of the wood, solemn days and wasted.

All night now
sometimes what I remember…

XXXII

The truths, all three, three sad lisps
on a small scale.
Any apprehensive could count them:
Totoes, root vegable, left over pages, spaper,

sweeping pulp from the roon, hirowgliffs.
Glib, glidder, out of luck.
Luck has everything to do with fatal diseases.

Skinnying.
Don't laugh at such cross-country skiers,
putting their arms in a game
with their legs, coldly
exploding from an old card game.

They speak cherry-laurel. Prettiful.
Take anaesthetics.
Drink the occasion passed.

Nitrous oxide! Solfatara!
The pompeiian dance continues
            beyond reaching your life.

Every truth is recorded
in fading ink.

Three hundred and fifty-six thousand million years
is personal.

XXXIII

Yet to arrive, I was greeted.
With the wonder if any of the drowning
could swim.
With a reciprocity listening for solidism
that could accommodate the world.

Alone, I killed the hermit.
With my bare hands, partial and unpromising,
wrested the germ cells
from the body of the universe, solo
and in the character of omicron
wove the two faces
into one devilic vision.
How lazy was the mirror returning my smile.
How goosey the flesh that resisted
                    the same flesh.

Life was good, unborn.
Sitting in the house, listening to the radio
in the J-curve of time.

Announcing the magic latent
in the subordinated segment of the population –
how those who do not exist are manifold.

XXXIV

It is impossible to 'pass through' this world.
Notice everyone like crows.
They are intense.
They are matters of passion.

When they tear they mean to tear.
Fruitfulness rends open their dreams.
Even slices, lumps, offcuts and scraps are determined.
Dirty feet are *de rigueur*.

My advice is gang up with them.
At the very least exercise your powers of love and purpose.
Unite a little piece of the universe with another bit.

Crawl into someone's side and legitimate the wound.
For it is impossible to 'pass through' this world.
Here, where everyone bleeds for a reason.

XXXV

Not being able to help it – this simple Christ sleeps.
And suddenly I wished they were all dead
so I didn't have to worry about the spaces
that I wasn't they were;

the ugly mosaics on the sides of brick buildings
and in my room a young man with one of those
Jesus Christ on the Cross guts which I thought ugly
until I saw one a week later on a movie
made stunning by the changing light and more eyes.
A screen you would one day tell me was too small
for a standard of living that slipped in and out of something
better than your parents once had and like them over time
we would become less able to speak outside the things
we didn't want to say.

Lazy and spiteful we walk to the pictures
(or maybe it is just sadness) when suddenly I remember
it is twelve years since we've fucked
but the way we get on… nobody would believe it.
When I bent over to go through the garbage on the street
you said 'Come on' and we lived in our own hard silence
your hand not touching my arm and only some memory
of impatience when seeing you fully dressed.

'Come on'
and I wonder why you care that I like
other people's junk perhaps it's the old men's eyes
late at bus stops

and the immorality of being willing to take
someone else's place.

Inside I hate your suffering new puritanical already
sleeping the way your stomach caves in away
from your chest with an ability to want
nothing and your hands nailed
arms stretched simply not
being able to help it;
you don't dream.

XXXVI

Beautiful mathematic.
She had no energy to deny
the effects of her beauty.
On this she counted
for it brought love
on its knees to her door.

And by the window
through which
she calculated the world
she saw hope going by.
Arms full of life.
Unnumbering realities.
Statistically she knew
it hadn't a hope
but there slonging.
Like this face
                    upturned
to her.
True as chaos.

Started out as a bunny rabbit
but didn't want to be a bunny rabbit.
Treated what was caught
in the brackets
as a malentendu.
Pricking the numb part of the voodoo
with her maker's dowel.

Wooden.
So now there's a head
where a head shouldn't be
on a chest that has had the wool
plucked from it

and a halter fitted.
Camel movements are relayed.

Make way for the convoy of economic sinners
artless on their engines!

XXXVII

The squares are shooting at me.
Three days they throw
as if a fourth might take up from there.
Corners making me presume even one.

A certain kind of geometry.
Two minutes from my career
someone following me
with the time.
How do you spell ghost?

'b' 'o' 't' 'h'?
I adored the boy who fell in love
with cruelty.
Who fourt the motor on his carpeted floor.

1–4 thoughts outside the square
and the circle fattens
like a word that confirms itself.

XXXVIII

The poem where the daughter
swallows whole the opal of her father
no longer waits to be written.
I wrote it. It returned bread. Circii.

What hurts is its pretence.
Authored by a pretender. This is not
on account of the audience members
who presume first-hand experience
but because of its non-poem kind.

Those who read it as poetry
have surrendered, have left
the labyrinth with the strategy
of language.
IN MY HAND
and in my heart never burned
they find the title always working.

Pass the word from animal to animal;
find the shock of narrative
eases their legitimate depression.
Eases their human hearts.

XXXIX

This poem borrows from my heart,
that closely huddling crowd
shouting out
now and then,
beating to death the lover,
blood running...

My blood   shooting the tourists,
supplicants to my liver and spleen,
years ploughing into my face
planting sorrows there,
the softest emotions of orchids
blooming in my teeth an industry of tears.

The three or four jobs held by my hands.
The cost of this mind that doesn't know
where it is from, cannot afford
the private tuition of the soul
(the alternative to this bankruptcy is murder).
Sleek green eyes wheeling around, riving
without a licence, skin ashamed and shook.

Worth of two lips to which the poem crawls up to see
if it will whisper its provocative body to the world!?

XL

Language as opposed to Friday to this day.
Are you a gladiator of the tongue?
Streetcornering your mouth-organ
in cheeky flap of ta tundastorm
like an impending wish the sound travelling
like demons as if lingua from dingua

rushing to the stung faces of those
who have hurried outdoors to catch
large drops of rain swallowing their own
chins while drinking the sky…
Singular blue of a plate
or some crying bird's breast…

Is this your moment-of … hyphenation?
Like the stillness (said before) of passion
in that moment of doubt
when loyalty dies.

Death warms as I leave the street for a house
following the only cloud to the rainbow's end.
Its phantom walls the beginning-and-ending-tale

of my storm in full swing like a happy party
in a dangerous mood…
It's hear without fear I raise my glass and toast
the tricky differences of this life
which usually scream pain…
To this world, the tunnelend's light…

XLI

The uprooting of words
took place here
in the country
with no tongue.

The most silent of plants grows here.
It is an animal that turns its belly
to the blade
and faces with the heart's generic face
the flower that bears the cold,
the absence which remains
after every replacement.

I am the animal, the plant, the silence.
Where might
I bleed from
to impress your fifty words
for wound, your
language
of
blood?

XLII

The Law of Waiting. Here
– where nothing has arrived –
true glimpse of eternity.

    Resides
between your stomach and your chest.

    Lives its life as a quiet, attenuated ache.

    Noticing
everything outside itself and paying attention
to nothing. But its own enormity.

    Eats
always
all things.
Housing it in one's body is simply unbearable.

    But what a sweet death it dies.
(With a Lazarene
wink!)

    Impatient, Maya sweeps pine needles
from their season.
A strange child runs in circles.

    Again I see logic defied.
As in all of life.
Tree grows down to the earth of me.
I am slung.

Vivi and Agnès sweep night into the shadows
of their knives.

Bed waits like a free enlargement of God.

XLII

Who knows dawn's plea.
Its working relationship with the hobby.
Dawn slow though urgent. Drawn slowly
through you. Thousands disappearing forever. Struggling.
Dawn where killing comes to a halt?

Allday eyeopening embargoed.
Until its launch. Complimentary. Okayday.
Okey-dokey. The donkey's resilience
brings 500 years to a standstill. To a sandhill.
To a landfill.

Who knows who is buried there.
The undersurviving tribe. Those who lived
securing tomorrow to their children.
Campaign for dawn!
So much the better these tragedies and inspirations.
Do them!

XLIV

For this week only
we're having the piano reinforced.
Filled up with Indians
of indeterminate typos.

Hung from the verandah the keys
make a tinkling sound that frightens off
the native fauna.

It's a scary wild life
in which all operations outside the head
and its attachments
cost. Money hides everything
that's not distracted. (Spends. Spent. Unevolve.)

Swinging piano, invaded not conquered,
orchid-ears & tall poppies jazzify your lament.
And when your black hides falls, the foeaux-wallabies?

Well, they'll shit themselves on the track.

XLV

Knowing the sea is how
paradigm unchastes the virgin.

Distant volumes expand as you approach.
The solar blanket is a song
that sings us all. Drops with parachutes
of desire onto canimals
and pecked birds alike.

Later than it really is, I sense
with disordered hearing the tearing
hearts of Anthology & Cleopatra.
Love is defluent and kiwi fruit halve spontaneously
to leave children with wing-buds.
Ibsen was one. Hatched. The only who understood
begetting from a wing is single.

XLVI

Scraps of paper and odds and ends,
bits and bobs are served to us
as the great feast of a false vision,
a deathless composition to be chewed blindly.

Split into thin layers, like poor authors
we pretend to be humble, press
refusal into cakes left for those we negate,
bargain again with the bad cook.

Rhetors come from the kitchen
with net bags through which everything
falls into not either and not nor yet not at all.

Our hunger could hew even the extreme
silent answer but there is no way
to take the nonesses in our mouths.

XLVII

My grave is in the high orchard.
How many years following my mother's death
was I born? Dry, crying,
her hands learn the inside of my heart

as if the world wants to fall in love
                              with its emptiness.
Planted among her I receive the bruises of her fruit.
When my body leaves hers it measures
the distance from her belly and chest and lights itself
from the fire in her eyes.

Though from ground nothing crawls out of, I rise
from oblivion and break the clouds.
Blood that ran from her navel fills the vessel
in which I begin to collect my life; which I use to bear
my imperceptible self to my tenuous self.

I sit on a rock. The trees have an edge.
They are naked. Your mother is why you die.
In a voice without restraint I ask *Show me something perfect.*
So perfect that I can understand myself what it is
and no longer need your sacrifice and distinction.

She smiles the smile she has, the smile,
and curiously I understand.
It is good to ask someone with so little.
Someone who has given all of you to yourself.

XLVIII

I yearn for more of myself.
My heart is a tiny bite.
Taken from the world.
The world tastes of yearning.
For the heart.
                    Most people stop
when they get to themselves.

    As if being is an insurmountable barrier.
Over-numbered, symbolic
of a kink, cloud-born.
Without opinion, my number is one. (I read myself.)

    This could strip every last word out of me.
Nothing would be left but the images I would show
was I not restricted to speech.
Description, numberless, then, I'm so boring
back here with my two eyes
and a brain that would *do that*
                    to the world.

XLIX

The office, anxious to find the ruin
of the trees, has a window.
　　　　　Inside
the stained plate critters with a piece of torn
flesh at the workday's
　　　　　　　centre.

　　The office-girl is on the bus passing
through the keyhole of today
　　　　　when?
they had whispered what
they would like to do to her
　　　　　　　in order to show her
　　　　　　　where she fits.

　　All the way she is still and silent, only
her breath swaying like some dry stalk in a
　　　　　　　breeze.
Some days the bread in her fingers sings
with tears to god laughing in the cafeteria.
　　　　　　　She stacks her thoughts.

　　And avoids their eyes, their panhandles
　　　　　　　between her legs.
She comes and goes and types
the soporific pastie of Monday, all-across-
　　　　　　　the-board of Mondays.

　　Cyclops whispers his storm to the door
while sphinx lays hard-boiled equality eggs
　　　　　　　in a foam cup.
More slipping down.

Albumen of the week glistening
in the starelight, smelling like the bluest eye.
Golf clubs falling from her womb
                    right into the poor week.
Then, like a woman with a sudden glassed head,
she stretches her insignificant wings and fries
right over last night's tragedy.

L

Nobody remembers the name
of the grinning padlock that girds
a woman's hips and fits
perfectly.

Commonly pharmaceutical is how
the dead are kept within the body these days
as the days, though still daily for the living, seem,
as seeming goes, a tad out of the ordinary.
(It is virtually the duty of an epoch
to intrigue its participants in order
that they not massly abscond.)

For example, understand virtuously
her forcely closed loins and you'll have missed
the index finger running
politically off with a column
of silver flames.
Don't just bleat
and scream,
all that bunk about history contains some um.

Say it! Mouth-Breeder, while you've hooked a minute's tail.
Some things I say, sly in the blood –
waiting for that moment
when the baby word cries out
.... !
I carry these young in my mouth for their protection.
But what is inside what?

LI

Hit or killed.
cycle suits cycle.
Seed turns
into sun(flower).

   Certainly doesn't lie.
All the castles' doors
are locked on the outside.
No-one knows what's on the outside.

   The crying-reasons of children
are different,
their methods of producing tears
are different.
As regards sound, tolerance
is attached to ownership.
Others' kids, you're deaved.

   It's hard to know what to do with a reaction
because all reactions are amoral.
Next time try subjecting it to centrifugal force.

LII

There are many things calling
out to me today, a truck unloading soil,
changeable weather, the unknown noise
from the narrow street, the masts
of two branches sharing a cobweb sail –
their call is like a finger to a lip –
and the sun with its burning sound,

mothers inspecting their children's shoulders –
twisting their heads like tossed leaves
to see their own,
capping a city
and writing a doctrine of sky –
                    in it there is only one
queen –
            all the other women have nothing.

In my window-box the fringed geranium –
floral fires – singe the edge
            of my view.
        do I see
            what is calling?
Long fingers of sound,
snug in the pocket of my ear,
in and then out and both at once.
A single petal –

yellow and red and purple
colliding with the soft rim
of the day,
cuddling hues sliding on colour
from one end of itself

to the other.
A million tiny insects crawl
between ten free stamens as the instant splits,
unshackled by the present,
through my fingers – now stays.

LIII

One hundred o'clock!
A bird grasps something made and asks
'Is this for people?'

I can't be a poet today – the world
keeps stripping itself from my body
and the bird keeps pecking
at the 360 degree skull of my roof.
Did anyone know the clocks would keep
so much time that we would lose our ability
to read them?

At one hundred and one o'clock
we bird-drop dead on the floor of imagination.
So the people whose ancestors were not there.
The worm-people, the nu, the first
officers of the same and gambits
involved in the full extent.

When we first began to measure it
did we understand time?
Was there an instant in which
later turned to face us
and we saw that it was what we had made?

LIV

Madness is a glorious membrary.
Envying how you left yourself.
Went out into the tiny other beings
and glistened like gangrene.

Grammar there's specialer.
Snuck and snuck and snuck.
Now in sane there's simply post-junta's
stripped curfew. All your outlaws
asking after you in the bars,
housefighting in the streets,
painless in the contamination
of their acceptance.

Some day soon it might be possible
to dump the rational and get again raw.
But you'll have to lose first.

LV

Boyle had jotted down somewhere that the day always begins elsewhere.

Cronin writes rapidly of strangling justice because there is an every-day that never passes beyond the sheep's noses. Who's the fairest? The white flocks remain unidentifiable, like blossoms that huddle to the tree for fear of a wind that empties like distance into their open throats.

Three times it was Wednesday as Wednesday lingers in the faithful old week. The name begins to spell itself backwards in search of a mate, the old pallordromes no longer useful as guides in such a world,
            a world of zombies with mollusclike mouths,
a world invented for the pure use of hope.

My unborn son bothers me again.
He is aging me and remaining stationary.
When I look deeply into the space he might occupy
I observe all the pages that have been turned upside-down.
There a citizen reads the impossible banning of reality.

Before us, suddenly, takes place the battle of the dimples.
A series of Buddhas comes bearing
the amberella chutney
while I crawl to the cupboard of flexible possession
            and slip through.....................................
                                                its jaw.

LVI

Breakfast is evidence.
For this reason I do not eat it.
Not only do I not swallow it, I do not prepare it.
In the night that chases the breakfast
I cover its tracks and protect my future
from jail.
My essential unseriousness cannot countenance cereal.

As a child I was told, "You'll blow up and bust"
                    And, oh, I busted
many times over before taking all the early-
morning reallys and dumping them
into the smallness of now
where there is credit in harm to oneself
as an alternative to leaning on ritual.

Our current leader has his face in a chocolate bar,
eyebrows made of the same
                    neutrality
that's been always claimed,
mouth like a set of tools for followers.

Identity after identity, cultureless.
Silent bomb after bomb exploding in the heart.

LVII

Second-classing myself, writing blah blah
to the newspapers because I'm sure I've the wound
from a boar's tusk, because in habits champagne
uninhibits the slap-happy bits.

I ask no questions about betrayal. Magritte
moved to Paris, Renoir died. All
existed under the double banner
as must be so.

It is fashionable in this dayandage to talk
of loving oneself, though it sounds to me
like fitting yourself out: for a good fucking.

And yet, we keep trying
and don't dare admit there's a right to suicide
that could revolutionise who we merely are.
A hunger strike could do us good.

Piffle-poffle, waffle and truffles!

LVIII

Today I met a man the ants had spoken to
and the kookaburras.

The day before Pluto was discovered it was still there.
Who said Pluto and in what language?

Did they have cold fire in their spine, teeth that reached
all way around the idea of it?
I live in the Pluto world but many more than me
have lived in the world without it.

The ants are living in the world without it.
I resent being part of any community smaller than all
the people of earth; larger than any lover and chosen friends.

Kookaburras laugh at my choices; a child mimics them.
I include offspring in my resentment.
But if I don't listen to those glowing with yellow mathematics
I can look up and Pluto's about the size of my darling's assurance.

I strain to see.
There's really not much more than all the science of it.
Taking it in my arms I sleep with the usual terror and superfluity.

Pluto is tidally locked and doesn't let go of Charon all night.
Collecting significant data from darkness
I calculate the never-before-seen surface of a distant dream.

By morning I've smoothed out the raw images
and the ants and kookaburras shine their languages
towards me.
The Pluto world tends to blur edges;
blends together
small features sitting inside larger ones

I crouch in the solar system with my darling's last word
on my head like a bright polar cap.
Ground-based light curves around the earth's observations
while I search for anything that shifts against the backdrop of stars
because it is night again and the kookaburras have all stopped
laughing.

An ant whispers Who said Pluto and in what language?
After three separate searches I met a man who made a serendipitous
discovery: "Every day is the closest approach".

LIX

Gallant lovelily! Allergy
we all suffer from. The number
tattooed on each of us
cannot be burned
from the body.

Perching hinterlands and fluttering coastlines
alike, there will never be sufficient water
to irrigate the available emotions.
Not ever. And it doesn't matter.

Those here and those over there
choose their own lies to straddle and ride up
the lightpost where they cling
like rats surviving the ship.
How familiar we all are.
To Shakespeare.
To history's mother
who allowed us around to play.

Red drums might bang, spine
vertebrae drums that strum *these
are your people* – THEY ARE!
but I guarantee there is a law you'll still make.
A law that will harden and harden you into imitation.

LX

Signs to Salvation –
one on either side of the road, pointing in opposite directions.

I apply the brakes.
I put my foot on the accelerator.
The car spun into an open trench and my soul rose straight to Heaven.
Fallen away in a state of health after this decathlon,
I gather information from the astronauts and angels.
All those reduced in useless circumstance.

Horizons and waves flow out from their confined places
and begin to fill in the special charts, feed
the classic plants and find 24 hours that someone will concede.
The town nestles and the earth thrusts up her breast.
Unfortunately, like all, as soon as they makes homes, they fight.
Even leaving the marks of their hands on the sky
that kept stretching itself towards all that was tender.

LXI

Tonight they've finally released my head
from the steps – from the *between* – where all day
I'd stuck measuring the depth of nothingness.
A hollow and invisible horizon.

The dead dog – the one who wouldn't
have died *IF* we hadn't got the cat (though
the cat had nothing to do with his death)
– comes to lick the brackets away.
Thirty isn't enough years to make any difference
to the fact that I'm still standing on the kerb
holding my mother's hand.

Would he not have died?
Some roads never crossed.
NOse on the bONe my brother
blessed with the best love
this beast could offer.

My father had the cheap-as-dirt shovel
to set right what didn't know
its chance was lost.
Spade for two purposes:
finishing off
and finishing off what was finished off.
(We all hope
our hearts are where the pain is.)

Though relieved from ending
by naming every dog the same.
To call and keep on calling…

I called and called and no-one came
to find me bum-up on the stairs,
out back. The old dead dog was buried there,
beneath, so that every day we could go UP
and DOWN without giving the dead our thoughts.

LXII

LimbO
When I enter you it is with a hearted globe,
half meaning less leaving as a memoir of a memoir
                    ideal audiences yourself,
exposes building as a foolproof method
                    of counting the dead.

POt-maker
Hear(,-)say, what the clay says at the barrier of earth,
how it counts itself up into the satisfaction
of your hands and curvely eats
the guilt that we process as if it was apple-smell,
that pushes forward like a capillary urge.

ResOlutiOn
On the street you bleed from all the right places,
                    return everyday
for the authority you have to say it to my face.
The ache-back involves unfurling the ribbon
of coherence across the end of the race,
to put your face through it is to rotate into coincidence
with another plane, one where beauty beauty
beauty is the main punishment for the bone:
                    seeds nausea   love-lost love.

    It's not just gold!
It's not just status.
Decisions to live in pain precurse the creation.
If I have hurt you it is all out of life – this inability
to excavate myself – and nothing more.
More was the task.

LXIII

With a painted tongue the voice bird
has opened windows in the door
of the tree through which flee
all the senses and a hand full of fingers
like a dying palm, brown searching

for green in a belly-pit or a century that stood
for a million years
upon the floor of history...

How did light remember
to come this way?

Bearing the painter's eyes
in a bucket of colours filled
as well
with the shadows of the day?

The vision breaks into six
and impresses the sky with its longing.
There is heaviness at his feet; wood, again,
exhibiting the strength of decay.

LXIV

Boundary poets look to marry those who are born nowhere. Like my AustralianIrishPanamanian who came out on the craps table at sea.

At eighteen he was ungreen enough for conscription, a dizzy adult upon whose beautiful six-foot frame claims were being made. My love does not regret him making the sea less full, being a guess-
t.
He lives.
And in the quietness of my forests and fields he lives forever.

He fishes in me and for this must not be held responsible. After all, you would pay for a garden and not a poem. There is no reproof in conception and the alternate similarity we make is one of possible delights. The two kinds – spontaneous and unexpected – of happiness are secrets unsearchable. We endure the dimensions of our expanded hearts by accepting the chance.

Over   Over   And over

(Get over it!)

LXV

Yesterday I went to Camperdown.
I went to visit someone from the ward
– triple bypass –.
His shirt was open (to let it breathe, said his wife).

His chest was sown up, extensively and
left nothing to chance.
(28 pills a day he takes, said his wife.)
He spent five weeks in hospital and got out yesterday.
I looked at his face and breathing chest.
Lying around the house all day.
He couldn't do much.
(28 pills away from being dead I thought.)

Can't walk up the stairs
– the altitude –.
They – the wife and daughter,
spent all morning over the calendar
working out when he would take the pills.
They were very excited.
Drank from cups of coffee
and argued alot.

The mother managed to say "The doctor said"
37 more times than her daughter
and so got the upper hand.
28 pills 37 times.
He is still swallowing yesterday's pills today
and destiny awaits him behind the smokescreen.

And so I went to visit Randwick.
Went to slap the dead man's money
on a horse looking for the characteristics

of a good racer: 'long body, small feet, wide across
the chest, good-sized nostrils and a low heart beat'.

And that's it then, all bets are off.
That's it.

LXVI

Twenty-third of November, wish Number 34.

Well, one thing we did do was get older,
as if greedy for death
and what we remembered,
the taste;
not the meal itself.

But one thing I do remember
is his 34th birthday.
He came to my door knocking, like a goblin
inhabiting a mine –.
Who points out the presence of ore
by knocks.

I shone like gold under the light he wore
on his little hat.
I was smooth and cold
and he coughed on his underground tears

And he said I wish, I do wish Lillian,
that you had given me an instrument
for measuring the dust
in the air.

LXVII

I am leaving the city; you are coming to the city.
Our love is found all along the roads.
When, without meeting, we pass, there is a darkness
which finds its shape as the shadow

of my body on yours and yours on mine
and, as in nights which own our thoughts
and are home to our longing,
our teeth grow blood and ache,

the phrases within us gather into flocks
and reel and screech at the silence
which cannot be broken
because no sound here is recognized:

    'Don't you recognize the sky?'
"It is not my sky. It does not belong to me."
'What's on your lips?'
"Only the moon. The host of the sky."

    'Do you hold it up with your fingers?'
"I will swallow it."
'Your mouth is bigger than the ocean.'
I am coming to the city; you are leaving the city.

    The salt and fishes have come from the sea
and offered their crystals and scales to the darkness.
Our love is found all along the roads
though my body and yours

       will never meet.

LXVIII

For some, the fourth of July is personal.
Some have their days for years
before public appalls them.
Exist before existing.

The eye's present whether it can see
and each twenty-two
plus two its own cabal
overrunning the place at its own pace.

This week, for April-example (day one
more than there are hours), they like
to remember the dead and drag the children
into it because children are resigned
to celebration and dig trenches
like there was no tomorrow.

This is not about pleasing us as
                    all the dirty work's
already been done. Now it's just films
and none of it helps.
But you can't speak and you can't listen.
The sobbing chokoes are on the vine
and neither full pay or half pay
can stop them forcing
a look at the images supporting. (Every photographer's legit.)

As for how I feel about it, the eyes
with perhaps six weeks to offer?
s
e
d
I

m
e
n
t

LXIX

The sea says the sky was pure opal now.
Stay there, it says, I'm coming.
How without care and anxiety I seize and guard.

In my depths the prospector's daughter
is setting places underground,
setting in stone
the world's childhood.
Only in the sea are your oldest friends.
Only there are the wonderful planets
able to live at night
through the necessary unmovable fights.

Philosophy is a thumbs-up to this.
But not interested in fish for themselves.

Fisherfolk know this and so do not indulge
in the luxuries of those who live on the shore.
Give away their lobsters.

LXX

I am characteristic strictly applied. The metaphor before it grows into the cliché of an accepted language.

Everytime I'm out I create a soul, creepmouse, silent
and shrinking and half of death. The learned Lord Ordinary
I call my soul.

Inside its fate the cuckoo duck falls in urban love, monstrably in the
demi-jour first mentioned my demon lowers the world
to half-mast.
Interruptible sky. Sky broken by the doubts of my love.
Sky acquiescing to the weasel-cat of Funktion-Lust.
Make naked the underlying rocks that beckon us all.

Guard as much as possible the detail by which you are forfeited to
death and known as the dead. Apply your tongue only to the attractive
hearth or to its act of floating.

Do not tremble for universal love but only for the little wave that
buoys you to the next tract. Tremble like an animal that is tired and it runs.

LXXI

Our afterbirth consists almost entirely
of insecticides and rodenticides.

We settle, ourselves, at the bottom. The earth,
we tunnel her right. Glass. Glassss. Party party.
Daily daily daily. Seduce us with belief.
Our sect is axe-shaped for pleasure.

Se defendendo. In our eye is seated
our fear and among it all the threats
of the subject shifting blocks.
Relics are no longer like phantom limbs.
They're between the ad breaks.
Transplants, transconfusions, the knitting of human hair.

Party on lobotomy!
The deadline is flatline.
Apathy has been injected with what 'ups' it
without altering its state.
However, however… there are those
that won't stop thinking though now are asked
to also consider this on remote.

LXXII

For years the curtains have been dying.
Dying like three-dimensional Rubens.
Overthrowing exhaustion for the study of verse.

    I love them more than the white chair
cracking its knuckles to maintain something.
They are very out.
Unfortunately, they have a beyond,
a replete context.
The veins there run with bibles and studied cases.

    (Remember the intensity of being 'out of check'?)
One hand, even tired, frail, illness-tremble
could lift them away from their data.
And then the curtains' prayer would
tend to find symbolism everywhere.
Don't judge with your left-brain!

    Such an excellent friend as one who covers
your hawks deserves parole.
Offer the shroud the excess of your two-handled drinking cup.

LXXIII

No bone!
How is life to triumph without it?
A bone made out of brown paper –
mEAgRe & hEARty (soup) floods the workshop.

But even rebels do deals. The life
is a spiral challenged by the galaxies' corkscrew into its
transformation. Tinty.
I give myself goats.
I know all their lines. "Yes I didint" "No you did"??
But they pretend against absurdity
and due to the appeal of experts paint only giant images.

Genius means throwing away:
those sad lions that can be kept as pets
are just terrible cartoons.

LXXIV

A warning…
A door as high as two doors.

A mirror with its own reflection.
A sound hidden in the world,
the sleeping family around you,
terrifying heartbeats and sighs
that you might cease to listen for.
The place always foreign
because you were born into it.
'Hello' never enough – louder?!

A realization. A warning.
You are miserable! You laugh!
Food is good – tiny pimientos grilled in garlic and oil
and every year more pigment fading
from your skin and lines branching out
as if trees rising like smoke
– blow it away –
your life

in this small tall white room in Madrid.

LXXV

A private pig.

How adorably noxious you are to me. A scatterling. I took you up and the gallery opened its walls to the poorest of the city.

You explained to me how the critics would want to know what was behind it all as the instigator had woven his unthinkable life into what had nothing in common. I said that distinctions were distinctions. Like the small differences between the living and the dead that few seem to notice. A small matter of preservation.

The pig had a horrible accent. A brain like a cactus. A brain like an entrée. Draggy buttocks. There are few insults that exact anything. Love is the better trespasser. "Absolutely not" we mutter to anyone that is worthless to our situation. And the latter is a little knocking fist on each other's doors. Open up to the euphemism!

The rest of them are inquiries. Turnip-shaped. Caught in the demand. Perpetually discovering lies on the longest day of the year and finding their horses burgled. Inside them it is typically spare. Furnished only by the boredom and the loneliness that is bought by selling one's flesh to alienation. The face of preparation is permanently turned away. Both ends of the devil trouble them.

And here at the exhibition the phone takes three lots of money in exchange for a whispered voice. "Step back."

"You smell."

LXXVI

Child two has made child three
a bed in the bath. The first one laughs.

My 2nd name is tirasse. Grinding, though grid-
locked, I'm the pedal-coupler in this organ.

I've more than one heartbeat which is why I am bent.
Water! Water! They're swimming! Footprints of blood.

This is the drama-day on which I know what
Adam means. What does Eve?
Sidekick or psychic? Sallet? Cold dish?

The sun personified? Fate to make.
Breakout again. Disengage the hackneyed.
These puny three will overpopulate the earth.

Simply with thoughts. Shhh. Are they detectable?
No-one in the story can hear the girl
only we can. She's moreborn. (*ecce signum*)

LXXVII

I look back into my footprints
for all that I know about walking –
the impression of love, the pressure
of the body in its lived past.

I imagine what if my footprints
impressed themselves on air
or became one day the shape of clouds –
all belief falling into that place
I have yet to put my foot,
everywhere

I have walked holding me
as I move its meaning toward
the single horizon that splits off suddenly
in seven directions
like something that is *not* a rainbow.
And it may be that on one of those old days
I passed a sign and for a moment was not myself
but all that is unrecollected –

and rain amongst rain.

Author's Comments on *A Ticket to Trilce*

I wrote *A Ticket to Trilce* almost 15 years ago and have not until now considered sending it to a publisher: *Sometime* is the right time. This does not mean that it should be published now but simply that I feel it's a good moment for it to have a go. The book was completed in several days – my poor memory asks me now if I was 'bedwritten' with a flu? – and was penned in response to reading a number of different translations of Vallejo's *Trilce*, including one by a friend and fellow poet, Peter Boyle. I love Vallejo's work, not just *Trilce*, but *Trilce* seemed to be asking me to respond, to converse, to talk. (Another work that had a similar effect on me was Neruda's *Book of Questions* in reply to which I wrote *Talking to Neruda's Questions* – published in Australia in 2001 and later translated into Italian and Spanish and published in Italy and Chile respectively.) The numbered pieces in *Ticket* follow the same in Vallejo's work and line-count, formatting, layout and 'mood' also seek the same ground. My book does, however, unfold very much in its own space and is by no means an attempt at 'comment' on the piece that inspired it.

What would I say about the book I have written: it is guttural, visceral, intuitive (perhaps moreso 'intuited'); it is quick, urgent and unapologetic. It is also a rational argument put nonsensically and thus a challenge to both the intelligence and the emotions. Its 'own cry', it therefore belongs to all who cry out – every truly owned utterance is owned by all. And it is kind of personal and because of this it doesn't *need* a reader. More than anything such a claim means it should be read. What is says does truly exist. I believe.

Reading *A Ticket to Trilce*

Cronin's remaking, re-envisaging, re-creation of César Vallejo's astonishing masterpiece *Trilce* enables a re-imagining of many of Vallejo's lifelong obsessions: childhood, the family unit, poverty, injustice and the anarchic joy of language. Just as in Vallejo there is an intimate self-exposure taking place alongside and within the disruption of language. The social structures that marginalise people and their experiences are seen as embodied in the language structures and conventions rigidified in traditional poetic and prosaic structures. Cronin, just like Vallejo, seeks to break both open. All the levels of life – the banal, the most elevated, the erotic, the pragmatic – collapse into each other. A joyous sense of multiple voices liberates the poetic from tired patterns: "All these things we use for walls / when the walls fall down!" (XVIII).

Much of Cronin's play with Vallejo's 1922 experimental sequence originates in the gender difference between herself and Vallejo and the humour to be found in male-centred assumptions. *A Ticket to Trilce* provides admission to a private female stocktake of an early 20th Century classic in a contemporary setting. A lover of Vallejo herself, Cronin provides us with a passport to another version of his great vision.

Peter Boyle
*(June 2020, after not having read
this work since it was first written)*

www.ingramcontent.com/pod-product-compliance
Lightning Source LLC
Chambersburg PA
CBHW022159080426
42734CB00006B/508

* 9 7 8 1 8 4 8 6 1 7 5 0 6 *